The Campus History Series

TALLULAH FALLS SCHOOL

Tallulah Falls Industrial School opened on July 12, 1909, with 21 students led by Annie Thrasher. As early as 1900, the Georgia Federation of Women's Clubs made a commitment to establish schools in rural areas of greatest need. During the school's earliest years, students from the surrounding area were provided with an education program that created generational upward mobility. (Courtesy of Tallulah Falls School archives.)

On the Cover: The first building to serve Tallulah Falls Industrial School students was dedicated on June 30, 1909, and is pictured here along with school officials including founder Mary Anne Lipscomb. (Courtesy of Tallulah Falls School archives.)

Cover Background: This group of students, pictured around 1929, gathered on the grounds of Tallulah Falls Industrial School. (Courtesy of Tallulah Falls School archives.)

The Campus History Series

TALLULAH FALLS SCHOOL

E. LANE GRESHAM

FOREWORD BY DR. LARRY A. PEEVY

ARCADIA PUBLISHING

ISBN 978-1-4671-0781-5

Published by Arcadia Publishing
Charleston, South Carolina

Printed in the United States of America

Library of Congress Control Number: 2021952810

For all general information, please contact Arcadia Publishing:
Telephone 843-853-2070
Fax 843-853-0044
E-mail sales@arcadiapublishing.com
For customer service and orders:
Toll-Free 1-888-313-2665

Visit us on the Internet at www.arcadiapublishing.com

For Joseph, Jackson, and Perry,
whose educational journeys continue to inspire me.

CONTENTS

Foreword

Recording the rich history of our school is an ever-evolving project. The number of stories grows by the number of graduates—every student represents a chapter in the Tallulah Falls School (TFS) narrative. Prior to this volume of words and images, former English teacher Carol Stevens Hancock penned an extensive work telling of the founding, initial growth, and history of the school's first six decades, starting with the 1909 opening of Tallulah Falls Industrial School.

Bringing to life this update to our school's story is the task of director of communications and media E. Lane Gresham, whose passion for local history is well established; her love for this place is evident in her commitment to sharing the everyday stories of this remarkable learning community.

This update provides an overview of those early years but adds to the story the exponential growth over the past two decades, when a shift in the structure and honing of the mission led to the school's current reputation as a top-quality college-preparatory school.

When my wife, Dinah, and I first visited TFS in 2006, we discovered a learning community with a wonderful mission that was not reaching its full potential. After retiring from Georgia College and accepting an invitation to serve Georgia Military College (GMC) as the vice president of enrollment and retention, I was enjoying my role at GMC and living in Milledgeville, where we had many friends and connections. Dinah and I were surprised at how much we were attracted to the beautiful TFS campus and the students. Even though we found it extremely challenging, we both understood that life has a way of shifting courses to reveal another path.

In the spring of 2007, along with the support of senior staff and the TFS board of trustees, we set out to change the trajectory of the school from that of a basic boarding school to one that is known across the state and region as an outstanding academic college-prep school that has the development of character as an equal part of its mission. During the past 15 years, we have grown by over 400 students and constructed more than $40 million in new improvements on campus. We have been incredibly fortunate to be presented with new leadership roles and be part of a mission impacting thousands of lives. I hope you will agree this volume captures both the past and more recent history of TFS, including its limitless potential for the future.

—Dr. Larry A. Peevy
President and Head of Tallulah Falls School

ACKNOWLEDGMENTS

The view from the window on the ground floor of the Willet Building offers a glimpse at what students in 1909 would have seen from their schoolhouse window. From my cozy office, I can easily imagine campus life from those earliest days of instruction. I breathe in the history of this place on a daily basis. To that end, I am eager to share a fresh collection of words and images to remind us of the storied history of Tallulah Falls School (TFS).

TFS is a place where children come to build a bright future.

TFS is a place where teachers commit to guiding students.

TFS is a place where dedicated staff arrive each day to contribute to the lives of these students. Our mission is clear—we prepare students to thrive in life by elevating character and intellect in a challenging and diverse college-preparatory environment.

My sincere appreciation goes to the president and head of TFS, Dr. Larry A. Peevy, for granting his blessing for this project; it has been many decades since Carol Stevens Hancock wrote her book about the first six decades of the school's history.

Thanks, too, to executive director for advancement Sonya Smith for encouraging me to stretch my storytelling in new ways and for her precise editing skills.

My coworkers in the Willet Building share my love for this place; I am greatly indebted to them for investing in this rarified, collegial atmosphere—they make my work life extraordinary.

And to our teachers and students whose stories inspire me daily—as the primary storyteller for this learning community, it is truly my honor to create compelling content as we continue to add to the collective timeline.

My gratitude extends to those who created, collected, and archived the school's image gallery throughout the years. The images are what make this project so compelling. What a treat it has been to piece together tidbits of text and weave the words together with the images!

And to my husband, Bill Gresham, who purchased the laptop that absorbed my first published stories all those years ago, I am grateful for his unwavering support.

Unless otherwise noted, all images appear courtesy of Tallulah Falls School.

INTRODUCTION

From the seeds of learning sparked on the front porch of a mountain cabin to the launch of a much-needed educational institution several years later, the origin story of Tallulah Falls School is a testament to the ability of one woman to rally an entire state to a common cause. Mary Ann Lipscomb saw a need for education among the children living in the remote mountain area near Tallulah Falls, Georgia. While she was a member of the Athens Woman's Club and president of the Georgia Federation of Women's Clubs (GFWC), Lipscomb launched a campaign in 1906 to raise money to start a school.

Opened in September 1909 with 21 students, the school is thriving today under the leadership of another educational maverick, Dr. Larry A. Peevy. The decades since those humble beginnings are marked by countless stories of individual successes with a common thread—the Tallulah Falls School experience.

On June 30, 1909, the Tallulah Falls Industrial School formally opened with a dedication attended by Lipscomb, woman's club members, local dignitaries, and families of the students whose lives would soon be transformed. Joining in the dedication exercises were Chancellor David C. Barrow of the State of Georgia and the school superintendents of Rabun and Habersham Counties. Ella Frances White of Athens and Passie Fenton Ottley, state chair of the Education Georgia Federation, were also present. State and county school authorities accepted the school for neighborhood use as offered by Lipscomb and Ottley. They promised to provide academic instruction, which the federated women of Georgia would supplement with the best industrial education.

The school's original building sat on five acres of land gifted to the school by Sara E. White. As the school opened its doors to the boys and girls of Habersham and Rabun Counties on July 12, 1909, teacher Annie Thrasher of Watkinsville, Georgia, welcomed 21 pupils. According to Rabun County Historical Society documents, one student recalled the first day of school as such: "It never occurred to us to question the fact that we were going to school during vacation time. We were happy to have a school building planned and built just for us."

It was not long before school leadership recognized the need for boarding accommodations. Because the school's location is in a somewhat isolated and mountainous area, transportation proved to be a challenge for many families.

At the February 4, 1909, board meeting, Bessie Willingham Tift, one of the school's trustees, proposed the construction of a cottage with lodging for teachers and 12 students. Within five minutes, board members donated the lumber, brick, lime, and a sum of money for its construction. The cottage was completed in August, less than three months from the time the work began. Architect Fred Orr had donated the design, and J.A. Saye was the builder; both men were based in Athens. The total cost of construction, including an estimate for donated materials, was $3,574.37. The building was named for Lipscomb, who served as the school's first director from 1909 to 1914.

According to National Register of Historic Places nomination documents, the one-and-a-half-story cottage was designed by Orr. Its low-pitched gable roof with exposed rafters and dormers, massive porch expanding across the entire length of the building, and the deliberate effort to use natural materials—rough cobblestone, exposed timbers and stucco in gables, and dark stains—make this an early Craftsman-influenced building. It is significant because it served as the basis for a philosophy that would influence the design of all the campus buildings that would follow it through 1946.

This second major construction project, along with the original Willett School building and those that followed, continues to influence the aesthetic of today's TFS. Modern-day facilities—including the Lucy A. Willard Middle School Academic Complex, Larry A. Peevy Upper School Academic Complex, Student Activity Center, and most recently, the natatorium—echo those same architectural elements. This thoughtful, consistent approach illustrates a visible commitment to the past while continuing to meet the needs of the modern student.

Like those early structures, the legacy of Tallulah Falls School was established on a solid foundation, with its "Light in the Mountains" still shining brightly for families of motivated students seeking an affordable, first-class education to prepare them for college.

After evolving on the slopes of Cherokee Mountain, the school continues to create generational shifts for area families, much as it did in its earliest days. While Mary Ann Lipscomb dreamed of teaching the children of the mountains to read, today's TFS faculty and staff are preparing young leaders to navigate a global economy.

In this work honoring the school's founding by those determined woman's club members many years ago, it is essential to note the school's exponential growth over the past 15 years. In 2007, under the leadership of Dr. Peevy, TFS changed course with a reconstituted mission. It was still a school for motivated students from the local area, but it became singularly focused on a top-quality college-preparatory experience. To implement this ambitious plan, Dr. Peevy brought in key personnel. A thoughtful approach to enrollment management led to a diverse population of boarding students who came from across the globe to learn and play on the 500-acre campus so familiar to alumni. Historic buildings remain, but state-of-the-art facilities designed for the modern student experience have been added to the campus.

Today, we can reflect on the past and look ahead to a bright future with 100 percent of TFS graduates accepted to colleges and universities and earning millions of dollars in scholarships each year. Enrollment has grown from 120 in grades 6 through 12 in 2007 to more than 550 in grades 5 through 12 in 2021. With more than 70 percent of students receiving some portion of financial aid, tuition is affordable for students from all levels of financial ability, thus ensuring a wide range of demographics. Mary Ann Lipscomb and the other TFS pioneering educators would be proud of today's students, who personify the traditions and spirit that have become synonymous with the Light in the Mountains.

Indeed, much has changed over the school's rich 112-year history, but Tallulah Falls School remains student focused and mission driven—a winning combination for any school.

One

Learning Launches

Mary Ann Lipscomb's dream of creating a school for mountain children evolved into something remarkable; just five years after Tallulah Falls Industrial School opened in 1909 with 21 students, enrollment had more than quadrupled. By 1915, Tallulah Falls Industrial School (TFIS) had grown to 96 pupils, with 14 of them on scholarships.

Lucy Willet took on a leadership role in 1914, and it was not long before financial challenges arose. Cancellation of the Georgia Federation of Women's Clubs (GFWC) conference in 1917 due to World War I put a strain on the institution's viability. It cost $3,000 per year to run the school in those days. After Lipscomb's death, her children offered $5,000 annually for five years with the caveat that $25,000 be raised for the endowment fund for the following five years.

Statewide local tax laws enacted in 1919 meant that Georgia counties would be able to fund their schools, and in 1920, the state school superintendent recommended "the separation of the public school at Tallulah Falls from the Georgia Federation's Industrial School." However, some Rabun County families wanted to continue to send their children to TFIS; they paid the school in order to make this happen. TFIS served as both a public and private school for roughly the next 50 years.

Four TFIS circles of supporters were formed in 1927, including the Atlanta Young Matrons' Circle for TFIS, which continues to provide financial support to Tallulah Falls School today.

Under the leadership of Passie Fenton Ottley, the school raised money for expansion during what was known as the Greater Tallulah Movement. Ottley's plans bore fruit. On the 20th anniversary of TFIS's dedication, Ottley detailed the school's growth. In 1929, she shepherded the school's transition to having 11 buildings, 250 acres of land, 265 students (including 115 boarding students), and $80,000 in invested funds, as well as its establishment as an 11-grade, fully accredited high school.

After this push, the school began to attract students not only from the surrounding areas but from across Georgia. As the school's first graduating class began embarking on the future in 1928, traditions began to emerge—celebrating with the learning community, posing for photographs, and collecting diplomas with members of the GFWC in attendance continue today.

Athens resident Mary Ann Lipscomb, with the support of the Georgia Federation of Women's Clubs, launched the Tallulah Falls Industrial School for 21 mountain children eager for the chance to experience a quality education. Lipscomb, who was born in 1848, graduated with honors from the Lucy Cobb Institute in Athens in 1868.

Mary Ann Lipscomb remained committed to the school until her death on September 13, 1918. The school's mission evolved over time as it served as both a public and private institution. Academics and preparation for life remain at the heart of the Tallulah Falls School experience. The quality of the college-preparatory program and the success of students are priorities that form the foundation for the school.

Students at Tallulah Falls Industrial School studied on long benches in the early days before the school had desks for everyone. This was common throughout the mountain area, as school buildings were also used for other purposes in the community. Having desks (as opposed to benches) limited the alternate uses of the seating.

Tallulah Falls Industrial School began educating pupils for the first time on July 12, 1909, with 21 students. Annie Thrasher is shown on the first day of school. Local families were so eager for the school to open that they did not mind starting in the middle of summer.

The growth of Tallulah Falls Industrial School is illustrated in this 1929 image of students gathered on the grounds. Also visible are some of the native rock walls that still mark the campus today.

This image demonstrates the commitment that families made in getting their children to school during the early decades of Tallulah Falls School Industrial School. The school's initial mission to educate children from the surrounding area required a partnership between families and the school.

Sara White donated the original five acres used to establish the school on the slopes of Cherokee Mountain in rural northeast Georgia. White, whose father was an early Tallulah Falls settler, is buried in a small family cemetery located in front of the Larry A. Peevy Upper School Academic Complex.

This is the original Tallulah Falls Industrial School barn. For years, the school managed dairy cows. Milking and managing the livestock was part of the work program for students. The barn was located near the site of the current Larry A. Peevy Upper School Academic Complex.

Lucy Sloan is pictured creating a rug. The original caption on the photograph says: "A clever designer and weaver of rugs." It is believed that this photograph was taken on the porch of the Lipscomb Cottage around 1920.

This is an early musical ensemble at Tallulah Falls Industrial School. From left to right are Lloyd McCall, Grady Nixon, Gertrude Kilby, and Maud Ridley. The photograph was taken at the Hunnicutt Photo Studio in Tallulah Falls.

The first graduation ceremony at Tallulah Falls School took place in 1928. Anne C. Davis, the principal, recommended to the board of trustees 10 students for recognition, and under the authority of the State of Georgia, high school diplomas were issued. The 1928–1929 senior class is shown with sponsor Emma Hardman, wife of Georgia governor L.G. Hardman, and school trustees. From left to right are (first row) Marie Cannon of Tiger, Lassie English of Rabun Gap, Nelle Mathis of Jefferson, Anne Taylor of Clarkesville, Salome Norton of Rabun Gap, and Maude Pittman of Maysville; (second row) Cora Shirley of Hollywood, Ophelia Brady of Bowman, Bell Harvey of Tallulah Falls, Gussie Harvey of Tallulah Falls, and Felicia Taylor of Tallulah Falls.

This photograph was used on the paper cover of the 1975 history of Tallulah Falls School, *The Light in the Mountains*, by Carol Stevens Hancock. Hancock was an English teacher at the school.

The student body of Tallulah Falls Industrial School is shown in front of the first classroom building around the 1920s. It is evident the students took pride in their appearance. Several teachers are visible in the upper right corner of the image.

Passie Fenton Ottley was the director of Tallulah Falls Industrial School from 1922 to 1932. Eventually, her title was changed to chair of the board of directors for the school. She was responsible for launching the "Greater Tallulah" fundraising campaign and proved to be a capable leader for the young institution. During her term, the school established 25 $2,000 perpetual scholarships.

Annie Carrington Davis served as principal of Tallulah Falls Industrial School from 1915 to 1932. She was a dynamic woman who brought tremendous enthusiasm to the school. She turned down a teaching position at the College of William and Mary in Virginia to come to Tallulah Falls.

In 1924, school leadership added a crafts shop to offer space for students to learn the Appalachian crafts of weaving, rug-making, and basketry. Handwork, basketry, crocheting, and woodwork done by students were being sold in markets as far away as Washington, DC. Proceeds from the sales of student-created items added to the coffers of the school. Lucille Bellew is pictured here in the crafts shop; she would sit inside the large baskets to finish them. Nearly all of this material is native sedge grass or broom.

A candle wrapped with the school's name, Tallulah Falls Industrial School, and its tagline (Light in the Mountains) is placed at the top of this early school emblem with Georgia's state seal in the center, a spinning wheel representing the arts-and-crafts tradition, a cabin signifying the students' mountain heritage, and the outline of the state with Tallulah Falls marked in the upper right corner.

This brochure, published in 1927, features images made by Sarah Hunter Moss, daughter of Rufus Lafayette "R.L." Moss of Athens and Tallulah Falls. The Moss family held prominent positions in the state. Sarah Moss was a well-known commercial photographer and advocate for education and women's rights. R.L. Moss established one of the first hotels in Tallulah Falls, the Cliff House, which became one of the most popular lodging options in the resort town. (Courtesy of the Hargrett Rare Book and Manuscript Library at the University of Georgia.)

TALLULAH FALLS IND. SCHOOL, INC.

On Cherokee Mountain

OPENED—July, 1909, with one small school building and five acres.

THE GREATER TALLULAH—Dedicated June, 1925, consists of 30 acres of land and nine well equipped buildings of native stone and cypress and a swimming pool.

ENDOWMENT—Invested funds of $70,000.00.

SITUATION—On Tallulah Falls Railway (connecting with Southern) North Georgia Scenic Highlands, on line of Rabun and Habersham counties.

AIM—To raise up leaders among our mountain people to work in their own communities.

STUDENT BODY—200 children, all the day pupils of vicinity and 100 boys and girls from remote sections who live in School Home.

CURRICULUM—Academic (through 12th grade), Industrial (all work done by pupils), Domestic Science and Handcrafts.

FUNCTIONS with state school system (no other school near) and Smith-Hughes Vocational fund.

SUPPORT—These funds so far as they go, but largely from Federated Women's Clubs of Georgia and the friends of education in and out of the state.

NOT A CENT OF DEBT

FOUNDER AND FIRST DIRECTOR—

Mrs. M. A. Lipscomb

SECOND DIRECTOR—

Mrs. Hugh M. Willet

HONORARY PRESIDENT—

Mrs. S. B. C. Morgan

"Like a shrine perched high on the 'Hills of Habersham,' lifting its face up out of the dark blue of the mountain range to the heavenly-blue of the skies above—a bar of real gold scratched from the earth, rests Tallulah Falls School, symbol of hope, faith and happiness to the mountain children of North Georgia."

"MARIANNA"

"At Tallulah Falls School there are no servants; every pupil is a proud and happy worker. They learn to do well things needful in everyday life: cooking, cleaning, gardening, milking, masonry, carpentering, painting; and in mastering these, heads and hearts are trained along with hands. They learn spinning, weaving, sewing, basketry and sundry other crafts, through which are quickened the sense of beauty as well as skill of touch. As a matter of course they learn the essentials of the usual grammar and high school grades, and are given the key to the immortal treasures stored in good books. But the notable fact is that they are educated not in words merely, but in life; not in one capacity alone, but in all the powers of their being."—Atlanta Journal.

THANKSGIVING LETTER

The best dividends which the friends of the Tallulah Falls School can receive come to them from the hearts and minds of the young people who pass through their doors. One of our graduates (now teaching at Tallulah Falls) wrote last November from Berea College, where she was completing her normal course, the following letter, expressive of her appreciation of the school, the federated women who maintain the school and their splendid principal:

Berea College, Berea, Ky.

Dear Miss Davis:

We are just back from our Thanksgiving dinner where we had some very interesting talks and songs about Thanksgiving. I have just been thinking today of the many things I have to be thankful for, and among them all, stand out most in my mind, the privileges that I am having to make my life worth more, so that sometime I may be able to help other people. As I think of all these things my mind goes back to the time when you took my sisters and me into your school. I have often wondered what would have become of us four if we had not come to Tallulah when we did. I am afraid we girls don't show our appreciation for the many things that you are doing for us, as we should. When I think of your giving your life in loving service to our mountain people, a prayer always comes up in my heart for you and I pray too, that I may learn how to do some work that will help people to be better and live more efficient lives. I am certainly very thankful for our Tallulah school and the dear people that are making it possible for us to be in the school, there and here. I like Berea better this year than I did last even. I am studying hard and trying to make good in everything. **I want to be worthy of Tallulah Falls School.**

"The Light in the Mountains"

Tallulah Falls Industrial School, Inc.

TALLULAH FALLS, GA.

Miss Ann Carrington Davis, Principal.

OWNED BY GEORGIA FEDERATION OF WOMEN'S CLUBS. OPERATED UNDER ITS OWN CHARTER. ADMINISTERED BY A BOARD OF TRUSTEES.

A home School where boys and girls of our own blood and breed, shut off in the fastnesses of the Appalachian Highlands from the opportunities which education affords, are given a chance in life at a school which, beside its academic course, supplies to them instruction in Manual Arts, Horticulture, Handcrafts, Home Care and the duty of an American citizen toward GOD AND HOME AND NATIVE LAND.

Tallulah Falls Scholar Reading to Her Grandmother.

Trustee Headquarters, Atlanta, Ga.

Mrs. John K. Ottley .... President
3415 Peachtree Road, Atlanta, Ga.

Mrs. W. B. Price-Smith .... Treasurer
69 11th St., N. E., Atlanta, Ga.

Mrs. Price Gilbert .... Secretary
Wesley Road, Atlanta, Ga.

Mrs. Z. I. Fitzpatrick .. V-Pres. and Special Representative
3415 Peachtree Road, Atlanta, Ga.

Vice-Presidents

Mrs. Walter D. Lamar, Macon
Mrs. Wm. J. Vereen, Moultrie

This 1927 brochure is believed to be the first printed promotional piece for Tallulah Falls Industrial School. (Courtesy of the Hargrett Rare Book and Manuscript Library at the University of Georgia.)

THE SCHOOL BELONGS TO GEORGIA FEDERATION BUT THE CHILDREN BELONG TO US ALL.

ONE OF THE "LEAST OF THESE"

Marianna, a little half orphan girl of the North Georgia mountain, has gone to boarding school.

A few years ago when autumn was bursting into the gay tints of the season, after tramping highways and byways for sixteen miles, I chanced upon Marianna's home. There on a lone mountain side stood a log cabin almost miniature in size; windowless and dark. The zinnias and golden glow played merrily in the warmth of the September sun and soft breezes outside. Marianna peeped shyly through a knot hole in the cabin door, while six young brothers stretched their necks from behind a woodpile to see the stranger with a red cross on her hat, climb over the fence and move towards the house. The belled pine-rooter (hog) gave me the "once over" and away to the woods he went.

Marianna's mother was out for the day working at some odd jobs in the neighborhood, to earn a few pence to keep body and soul together in her family of fatherless children. I found under the roof of her humble cabin that an aged woman of seventy-six had been "adopted" who had no relations and no one to look to for support. The infirmities of old age—rheumatism, deafness and partial blindness had crept on. She was unable to work. Truly the widow's mite was shared for the cabin (with its two beds and seven children) was none too small to deny this woman, weak and old, the best to be had in it. After a few years with this family, she died. Sometimes we "entertain angels unawares" but in this instance—an angel was hostess.

Now, this widow has become homeless and, with her children scattered here and there, she sings daily over the washtub while little Marianna, thirteen years old, is being educated in boarding school. Not once has she referred to Marianna's education lifting herself from constant toil and drudgery. Her song and hope is only that Marianna may "get education" and be more to the world than she has chanced to be. With this wish in every fibre of her heart, she cheerfully bends her frail body over a tub of soiled clothes and sings her way through eternity. Although a loving, devoted mother, she has had to place her children out with her hard-pressed relations. Poverty forced her to separate even from her youngest. Meanwhile, Marianna, as she saw her first train pull into the station eighteen miles from home, timidly brushed a tear away and said: "I hope my learnin' 'll help me to do something for mama and my brothers." And, the train carried her on to Tallulah Falls Industrial School.

What shall we do for the six young brothers Marianna left behind? And for the many other "Mariannas" of this mountain region?

This story was written by Miss Margaret Harry, Delano Memorial Red Cross Nurse, stationed at Highlands, N. C., and covering Georgia as well as North Carolina territory. The Red Cross is furnishing this child with clothes, books and traveling expenses, while some unknown friend through Tallulah Falls School, is giving her a $150.00 scholarship.

As a result of this letter, two of Marianna's brothers are now in the school. But there are so many other "Marianna's"! WILL YOU NOT GIVE A SCHOLARSHIP OF $150.00 FOR ONE OF THESE AND JOIN US IN THIS WORK OF SALVAGING AMERICANS?

SCHOLARSHIP S. O. S.

One hundred girls and boys live in the School Home at Tallulah Falls. Nearly every young life holds a tragedy through which the school is helping them to live and develop.

We cannot let one child go and yet we have only half enough scholarships for them!

Will you not give a **chance in life** for one year to one of these children by the gift of $150.00 or

Establish a Perpetual Scholarship of $2,000.00 which will provide for one child for all time?

These Perpetual Scholarships carry a name. What a wonderful opportunity for immortality for yourself or for a loved one!

PERPETUAL SCHOLARSHIPS ($2,000.00 EACH) BEARING NAME CHOSEN BY DONOR

Salome Hanna Chapin Jones ... Mr. and Mrs. C. M. Chapin
Robert Towns Daniel ... Mrs. J. Sprole Lyons
Atlanta Debutantes of 1925.
Letitia Pate Evans ... Mrs. Kelly Evans
Gertrude Hanna Haskell ... Mrs. Coburn Haskell
Celeste S. Parrish ... By Vote Trustees
S. B. C. Morgan ... By Vote Trustee
Sarah E. White ... By vote Trustees
F. M. Robinson ... Mrs. F. M. Robinson
Birdie Cobb Smith ... Senator Hoke Smith
Donna Cappie Lewis Stone ... Mr. and Mrs. F. O. Stone
Jean Cochrane Witham ... Mrs. Rufus T. Dorsey
Laura Witham Dorsey ... W. S. Witham
Edith McGregor Adams ... Woman's Missionary Union, Highland Park, Ill., Presbyterian Church
Ada Reynolds Alexander ... Mrs. Jas. E. Hickey
Nannie Reynolds Maddox ... Mrs. Henry S. Jackson
American Legion, Atlanta Post No. 1.
Florence H. Brownell ... Mrs. F. H. Brownell
Atlanta Federation Founders' Scholarships:
Sallie Chase Pattillo—Frances Fort Brown
Dosia Head Brooks ... Mrs. R. P. Brooks
Annie Mae Broach ... Rhododendron Club of Atlanta
Nellie Peters Black
Mrs. Lamar Rucker and Mrs. John McDougald
Alexander W. Cawthon ... Mrs. C. K. Ayer
College Park Woman's Club:
Anne Graves—Sina Harris White
Georgia Elks' Association.
Elks, Atlanta Lodge No. 78.
G. J. Foreacre ... Mrs. Blewett Lee
Business and Professional Women's Clubs of Georgia:
Lena Lake Forrest
Arthur Otis Granger ... Mrs. A. O. Granger
Sarah Harper Heard ... Mrs. Jas. Y. Swift
Harriet Cordelia Dick Inman ... Mrs. Morris Brandon
Garner Jones ... Mrs. Felton Jones
Inez Wilkins Jones ... Mrs. I. W. Jones
Sarah Cornelia Lunquest ... Mrs. S. C. Lunquest
Ella Mitchell ... Washington County, Ga., Federation
Passie Fenton Ottley ... John K. Ottley
Ga. Assn. Ed. Ga. Mountaineers.
Anna Nowlan Thiot ... Mrs. Elizabeth T. Winship
Lucy Lester Willet ... Hugh M. Willet
Mary Ruth Dobbs ... Mrs. S. C. Dobbs
Evelyn Watson Patterson ... Mr. and Mrs. J. M. Patterson
William Jackson Keenan ... Mrs. B. K. Boyd

MARY ANN LIPSCOMB FUND

PASSIE FENTON OTTLEY FUND

LEWIS H. BECK FUND

Mrs. Bolling H. Jones, Chairman Memorials and Tributes.
Cherokee Road, Atlanta, Ga.

Called the "Niagara of the South" by newspapers across the country, Tallulah Falls and its gorge became a destination for tourists seeking fresh air and outdoor recreation. The group pictured here includes Tallulah Falls Industrial School founder Mary Ann Lipscomb (third from left in the back row).

The White siblings are shown outside the Lipscomb Cottage. These motherless children found a home at Tallulah Falls Industrial School in the 1920s. Clockwise from left to right are Edwin (14), Frank (11), Virginia (7), Mary (9), and Hugh (5). This image was featured on the cover of the Tallulah Falls School magazine to mark the school's centennial in 2008.

THE CONSTITUTION. ATLANTA, GA., SUNDAY, JULY 4, 1909.

WOMEN'S CLUB NEWS OF GEORGIA

A PAGE DEVOTED TO THE MANY INTERESTS OF GEORGIA'S GREAT ARMY OF CLUB WOMEN

DAUGHTERS OF THE AMERICAN REVOLUTION | GEORGIA FEDERATION OF WOMEN'S CLUBS | UNITED DAUGHTERS OF THE CONFEDERACY

MRS. SCOTT TO BE PRESENT AT BRUNSWICK CONFERENCE

TALLULAH FALLS INDUSTRIAL SCHOOL FORMALLY DEDICATED ON WEDNESDAY

TELEGRAMS.

PARTY ENTERTAINED BY MRS. LIPSCOMB

OFFICIAL NOTICE.

LETTER OF THANKS FROM PRES. SOULE

VETS AT SOLDIERS' HOME GIVE REMINISCENCES

JUNE MEETING OF DALTON CHAPTER

GENEALOGICAL

A NOTABLE MONUMENT.

TO MRS. CORNELIA BRANCH STONE.

GOD'S ACRE RECLAIMED.

CHEROKEE CLUB.

M'RAE, GA.

BREAK AWAY! From business cares and take a trip to the seashore—St. Simon, Cumberland—via Atlanta, Birmingham and Atlantic. Finest equipment—Pullman sleepers between Atlanta and Brunswick. Rates for long or short stays. City Ticket Office, 70 Peachtree.

SKIN BEAUTY

CUTICURA SOAP

In the treatment of affections of the skin and scalp, which torture, disfigure, itch, burn, scale and destroy the hair, as well as for preserving and purifying the complexion, hands and hair, Cuticura Soap and Cuticura Ointment are well-nigh infallible.

WEDEMEYER'S CONCERT BAND AND ORCHESTRA

Music Furnished For Concerts, Chatauquas, Fairs, Commencements, Receptions, Parades, Dances, Etc. Up-to-date Library of Music. ATLANTA, GEORGIA

SAMUEL G. WALKER PICTURES. ART STORE. KODAKS. Artists' Material, Picture Framing, Amateur Finishing and Supplies. 88 PEACHTREE ST.

Buy it once and you'll always use K K K flour.

Women's clubs across the state supported the formation of Tallulah Falls Industrial School. The clubs were often featured in the *Atlanta Constitution*. This July 4, 1909, edition of the newspaper notes the details of the formal dedication of the school.

Two

Challenges Conquered

A 1934 newspaper story written by Mildred Seydell in the *Atlanta Georgian* summed up 25 years of achievements: "The school is called the Light in the Mountains because ignorance is darkness and knowledge is light. . . . A small seed of a dream, it was planted; it prospered. Now, after 25 years, it has blossomed into the blessed beauty of an institution which is training boys and girls into upright, intelligent, happy, healthy men and women."

This season of growth for the school was bountiful. In 1937, the word "Industrial" was removed from the school's charter; by the 1930s, the term had come to be commonly used in the titles of incarceration facilities for youthful offenders, and this context was totally inappropriate for the Light in the Mountains. For the first time, the school became officially known as Tallulah Falls School (TFS).

World War II brought new challenges, including the scarcity of fuel and the tightness of money. Many of the "Tallulah boys" entered the armed services, and many, like Lt. Owen Lee Buford (class of 1939), would never return. Gifts of war bonds came in regularly. During the school's Christmas party in 1943, Ida Fitzpatrick announced to everyone that the US Treasury Department had decided to name a bomber airplane *Tallulah* in appreciation of the school.

Only a few months later, on March 1, 1944, disaster struck. The Willet House, the school's original building and central structure, was destroyed by fire. Work began almost immediately on raising funds to rebuild, and on December 13, 1946, the Lucy Lester Willet Community Building was dedicated.

By 1952, TFS had 130 day students and 118 boarding students. The school was accredited by the Southern Association of Colleges and Schools and certified with quality by the state board.

In February 1957, Nannie Woodward Westmoreland died and left her entire estate to Tallulah Falls School. The board of trustees passed a resolution to build the Nannie Woodward Westmoreland Dormitory, which could house 75 females.

"A Golden Age, A Golden Future" was the theme for celebrating the school's 50th anniversary in 1959.

Ida Fitzpatrick, known as the "Duchess of Tallulah," became director and resident trustee of the school in 1932. In 1934, the 25th anniversary of the school, the senior class sent its first Jubilee gift of $25 to the school trustees with the suggestion that "all friends of Tallulah make gifts this year in units of 25." Members of the Atlanta Young Matrons' Circle took the seniors' challenge to heart and raised $25,000 for the Jubilee.

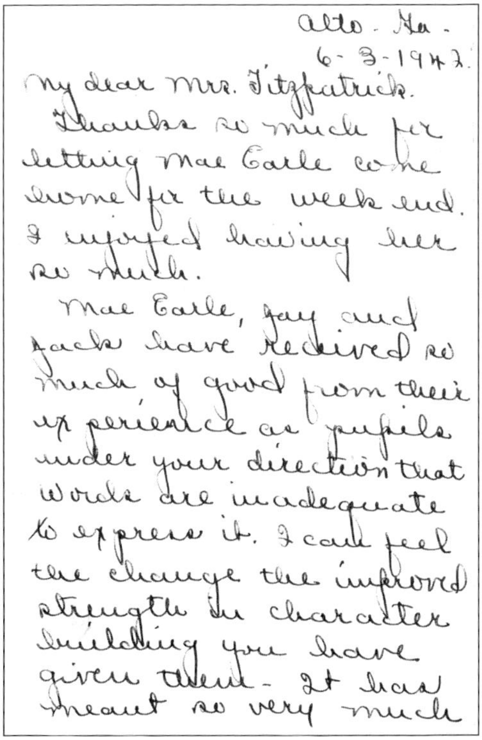

Alto. Ga.
6-3-1942.

My dear Mrs. Fitzpatrick.

Thanks so much for letting Mae Earle come home for the week end. I enjoyed having her so much.

Mae Earle, Jay and Jack have received so much of good from their experience as pupils under your direction that words are inadequate to express it. I can feel the change the improved strength in character building you have given them. It has meant so very much

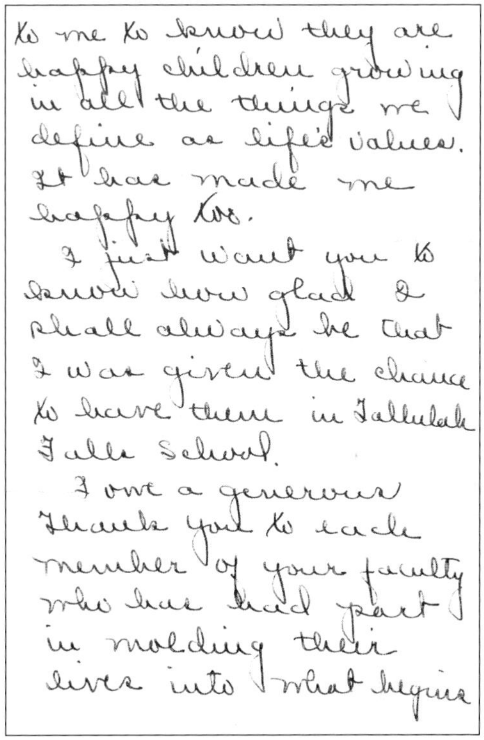

to me to know they are happy children growing in all the things we define as life's values. It has made me happy too.

I just want you to know how glad I shall always be that I was given the chance to have them in Tallulah Falls School.

I owe a generous thanks you to each member of your faculty who has had part in molding their lives into what begins

This 1942 letter from an area mother expresses gratitude for the educational experience of her three children. The mother wrote: "It has meant so very much to me to know they are happy children growing in all the things we define as life's values. It has made me happy too." The school's archives are full of such correspondence from grateful parents and guardians. During the early years of Tallulah Falls School, the school took in entire sibling groups who, due to various circumstances, were left without proper care in the family home. This mother's sentiments echo through generations of families whose children benefitted from the Tallulah Falls School experience.

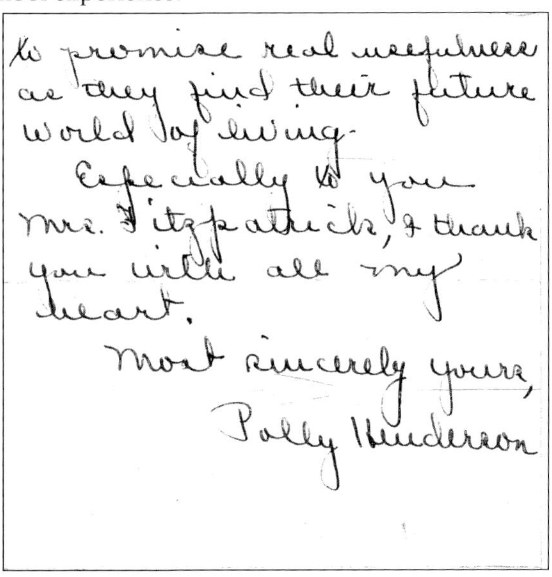

to promise real usefulness as they find their future world of living.

Especially to you Mrs. Fitzpatrick, I thank you with all my heart.

Most sincerely yours,

Polly Henderson

A new water supply resulted from the Greater Tallulah Campaign, an early fundraising campaign. A new pool named for Ida Fitzpatrick soon became a favorite spot for cooling off. It was located in the same location as the firepit at the current Circle Building.

Work was an integral part of the experience at Tallulah Falls Industrial School for two fundamental reasons. First, the school wanted its students to learn practical skills they could put to use back at home or in the world beyond. Second, the school depended on the crops and livestock that students helped to raise for food. Handwork, basketry, crocheting, and woodwork done by students were sold in markets as far away as Washington, DC. Pictured in the 1930s are, from left to right, Norma Waldrop, Maxine Smith, Betty Norton, Theresa Norton, Bobby Smith, Enid Waldrop, Marjorie McGee, and Edith Redding.

As the story goes, a local family needed a way to pay tuition for a child to attend Tallulah Falls Industrial School. Lacking money, they delivered a mule to the campus in exchange for an education. According to Walter Hunnicutt's story "The Legends of Tallulah," the mule was ridden onto the school grounds in September 1924 by two boys who asked if they could "give the mule to Tallulah for their education." The deal was gladly accepted, and Frank Tallulah did much heavy lifting for several decades, carting down big rocks for new buildings from the slopes of nearby mountains as well as helping with garden and field work for the school. Frank Tallulah, pressed into service at the school's farm, made an impact and provided a whimsical touchstone for students. For several years prior to his death in 1951, Frank Tallulah enjoyed a comfortable retirement as the school mascot and an adored student companion.

This maintenance crew from the school's early days consisted of Robert "Uncle Bob" Williams and Frank Moore, with mule Frank Tallulah providing the horsepower. It appears they are hauling supplies—perhaps rocks or logs from the surrounding area.

Dr. Glenville Giddings built this clinic, known as the Giddings Cottage, in 1931 so that he could study the children who drank Coca-Cola in the evening, which attracted much attention from the medical profession. The structure was a one-and-a-half-story Craftsman-influenced building with a fieldstone basement and a clapboard-sided first floor.

Dr. Glenville Giddings reportedly found that hot chocolate had a more dramatic effect on children than Coca-Cola. At one time, this building had a dormitory for girls and one for boys, each with a capacity of 12, as well as three teachers' rooms, baths, and a little sitting room. Dr. Giddings was the son-in-law of Preston Arkwright of Georgia Power. This building also served as classroom space and currently houses the school's archives.

The children who were part of Dr. Glenville Giddings's study are pictured here. They are, from left to right, (first row) Sarah Hoffler; (second row) Joan Rickman, Ella Lee Wilbanks, Clyde Stancil, and Willie Lee Patterson; (third row) Bobby Calenback, Ruth Hills, and Evelyn Stewart; (fourth row) Robert Walker Jr., Jess Rickman Jr., Dorothy Cadell, and Clara Hicks; (fifth row) Van Vickery, Kitty Hopper, Eugene Baron, Odilla Bray, June Teague, Riley Garland, Wayne Wiley, and Louise Wiley.

In 1934, newspaper editor and writer Arthur Brisbane wrote an article about his visit to the Light in the Mountains for his syndicated column, Today, which was read by 40 million people across the world. Brisbane wrote: "If any man who has let his heart grow hard in the struggle against other men would like to feel as a man should feel once more before he dies, let him go to that school in the mountains of Georgia and see the children. . . . Emotion you feel as you have not felt for many years, not since the days when life seemed real and everything seemed possible." Dan Smith, a well-known American newspaper illustrator from Philadelphia, created this painting—*The Light in the Mountains*—in 1925. The model in the painting is said to be Eliza Shirley, a student who showed so much promise that Anne Davis took her to Lynchburg and New York to receive additional training in weaving and other industrial arts.

Gray Eagle was reported as being the last of the Cherokee chiefs. His chair—which was hewn from a single stone and weighs over 500 pounds—was loaned to the school by the Adam Vandiver family; it was reported that Vandiver's grandfather sat in council with Gray Eagle in 1835. Local lore says the chair cannot be given away; it can only be loaned. The chair occupied a place of prominence on campus near the Willet Building.

The last official use of Cherokee chief Gray Eagle's chair is said to have been by the chief on the day the federal government forced the Cherokee people to leave their homelands in Georgia and begin their travels on the Trail of Tears. Stories about the chair and its origins vary, but it is confirmed that Gray Eagle's family members asked for it to be returned. Although Gray Eagle's chair once sat on the school's campus, its current location is not known.

In the early days of Tallulah Falls School, students were taught life skills. This trio of students was enrolled in the school's domestic science class. An evolution of sorts has taken place, with culinary arts now a popular elective choice for students. Pictured here are Blanche Warren (left), Adele Seabolt (center), and Ethel Moore.

One of the school's more unusual artifacts is a vintage courting bench. This is one of many furniture pieces that was handcrafted using natural materials that are plentiful in the area. This particular style evokes the Adirondack style that originated in the Great Camps in the Adirondack Mountains area of Upstate New York.

A strong work ethic was instilled in the student body at Tallulah Falls School. This student is contributing to the daily operations of the school by sweeping a set of steps on campus. The fencing echoes the rustic Adirondack style, as do other areas on campus.

At one time, there were expansive rose arbors on campus. These were constructed of native wood and showcased hundreds of roses. Two of the school's original buildings are visible in the background of this image.

In what appears to be a precursor to the International Day celebrations introduced later in the school's history (and still honored today), this image illustrates the school's commitment to educating students about what the world is like beyond the Appalachian region.

There is a strong interconnection between Tallulah Falls School and the clubs from across the state that are part of the General Federation of Women's Clubs–Georgia (GFWC Georgia). At the time of the school's founding, this organization was known as the Georgia Federation of Women's Clubs. Mary Ann Lipscomb's impassioned plea to her fellow club members in the early 1900s was what led to the formation of the school. Today, GFWC Georgia club members support the school through financial means and through board representation. The state office is housed in the historic Lipscomb Cottage, which is located on the TFS campus. Ida Fitzpatrick is in the first row just left of the center.

Another season of handcrafts included spinning and weaving. Fannie Rogers is shown at the spinning wheel in the 1930s; her grandmother was one of the earliest helpers in spinning and weaving efforts at the school.

Student activities and entertainment are often mentioned by alumni when they are asked about their favorite memories of the school. The ground floor of the Willet Building, which now houses administrative offices, was used for dances, roller-skating, and other activities. This c. 1934 picture features a type of folk dance called a ring dance.

In May 1954, Kermett J. Harris took over the directorship of Tallulah Falls School, a move that resulted in 17 years of tremendous growth and well-being for the school. Funds for the Cannon Memorial Endowment became available in 1954 through the sale of the Henry Grady Hotel in Atlanta, and a planning committee was formed to guide and advise in the building program for the H.R. and C.R. Cannon Building. Today, the school's upper school academic complex renovation has transformed the original Cannon Building into a state-of-the-art, modern facility more than twice the size. It was during the 50th-anniversary celebration in 1959 that the H.R. and C.R. Cannon School Building and the Nannie Woodward Westmoreland Dormitory were dedicated.

The 1950s continued to be a time of growth and progress at the school after the accelerated expansion of buildings and physical improvements. Traditions, including white dresses for graduation (for the female students) and the outdoor school photograph, are among reflections from alumni. This image shows the Willet Building.

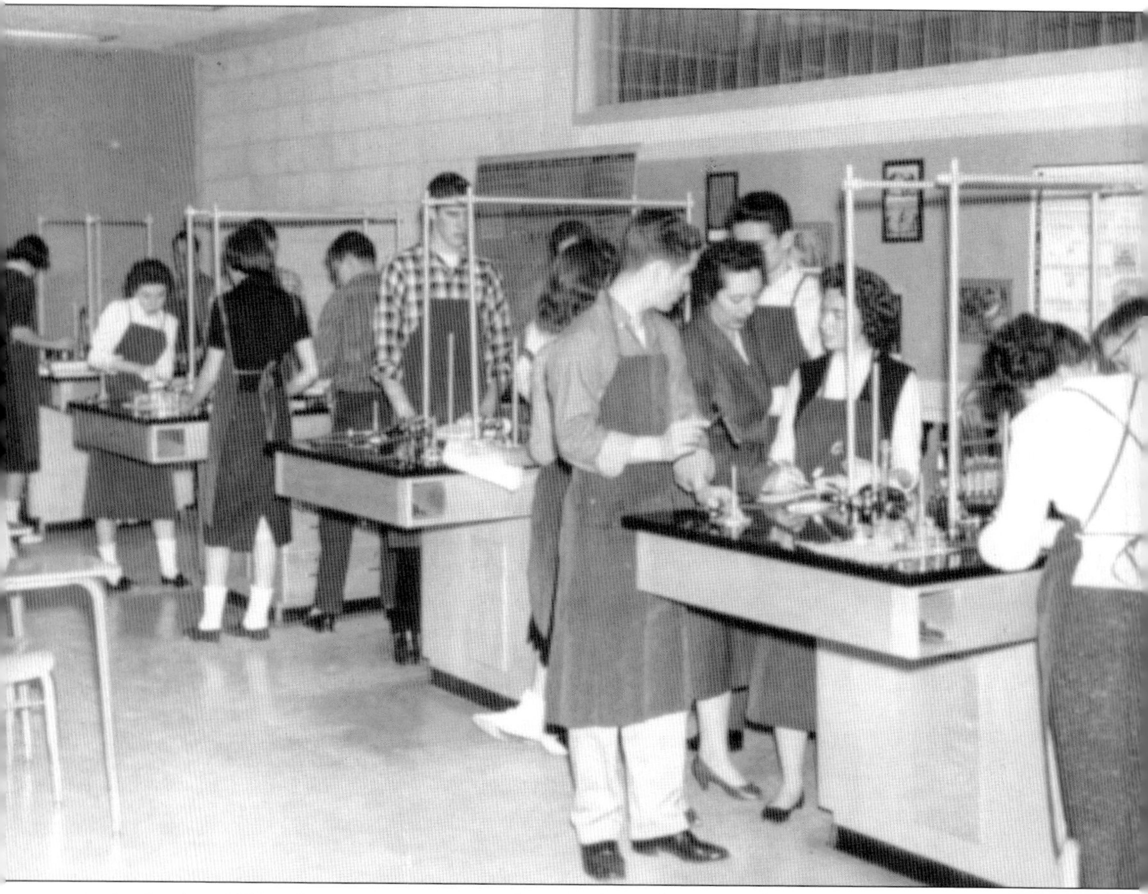

Later in the 1950s, classrooms were modernized, as shown in this image featuring a science lab. The school's facilities have continued to evolve to meet the needs of students.

In this 1950s image, a group of female students is shown posing in the basement of the Willet Building, which now houses the school's administrative offices. The Willet Building also once housed the former dining hall.

The Willet Building has served many purposes through the decades. The original Willet Building burned down in 1944 and was rebuilt to serve additional generations of students. The kitchen and dining room are now the business office and conference center, respectively. The original dinner bell is located just behind the building. These students, pictured in the 1940s or 1950s, are ready for a meal.

Fess Parker, an actor who portrayed Daniel Boone and Davey Crockett, was on location in the area for the 1956 Walt Disney film *The Great Locomotive Chase*. It was a thrill for Tallulah Falls School students to meet Parker and pose for a photograph. The handwritten note on this picture reads: "Hi gang, It was fun meeting you. And good luck to you in all things. Fess Parker."

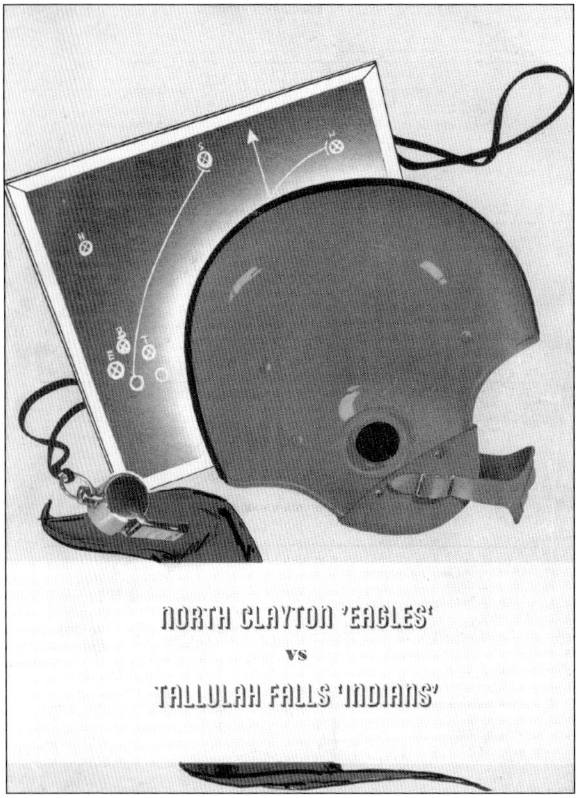

A group of alumni from the early 1950s fondly recalled playing football for Tallulah Falls School. The late Herb Amick launched the program; he served as a coach and athletic director from 1953 to 1957. The team had quite the record for several years. Coach Amick dubbed the 1953 team the "Scrappy Bunch." The school's win-loss records for 1956 and 1957 are 6-4 and 7-3, respectively. The soccer field, dedicated in 2015, is named for Coach Amick.

Three

Transitional Times

Beginning with the 1970–1971 school year, after much correspondence and planning with the Georgia State Board of Education, Tallulah Falls School (TFS) became a privately chartered institution and no longer accepted public funds for its operation. For accreditation reasons, the school discontinued grades one through seven.

Dr. Franklin Shumake became president of TFS in 1971. On May 13 of that year, Gov. (later president) Jimmy Carter was the keynote speaker for the dedication of the Young Matrons' Circle Building, a multiuse facility. The Mary Ann Lipscomb Building was also dedicated that day. The original Lipscomb Cottage, the first dormitory at the school, was restored and served for several years as the president's office and the school museum. The first international students came to TFS during the 1972–1973 school year. In 2021, the school served approximately 80 international students from more than 20 countries.

The first annual Homecoming Day was held on Sunday, May 6, 1973. Efforts were made through various media channels to reach as many of the estimated 20,000 former TFS students as possible. Alumni present at that first homecoming had attended the school as far back as 1909, when the school opened. All 600 attendees enjoyed a day of tours, food, and remembrances.

During homecoming in 1984, ten outstanding former students were chosen from among those who had attended the school since 1909. The alumni association continues to honor outstanding former students each year.

In honor of Christa McAuliffe, the schoolteacher who died in the 1986 *Challenger* accident, Congress directed schoolchildren to name the orbiter being built to replace the *Challenger*. The nine-student team at TFS named the shuttle *Endeavour* after the vessel used by Capt. James Cook in his 18th-century sea explorations. More than 6,000 entries were submitted in two divisions, secondary and elementary; TFS won on the secondary level. Pres. George H.W. Bush presented an award to the TFS students on May 16, 1989, in a ceremony at the White House. Each year, TFS students travel to the Space Coast of Florida to learn more about the space program and have lunch with an astronaut.

Dr. Franklin Shumake became president of Tallulah Falls School in 1970. The complete list of school leadership is as follows: Mary Ann Lipscomb, director (1909–1914); Lucy Lester Willet, director (1914–1922); Passie Fenton Ottley, director (1922–1932); Ida Fitzpatrick, director and resident trustee (1932–1951); Dr. J.C. Rogers, director (1951–1953); Kermett J. Harris, director (1953–1970); Dr. Franklin Shumake, president (1970–1988); Dr. Charles Green, president (1989–2001); Dr. Gary Coker, president (2001–2002); Dr. Kent Anglin, president (2002–2006); and Dr. Larry A. Peevy, president (2007–present).

On May 13, 1971, Georgia governor Jimmy Carter was the keynote speaker for the dedication of the Young Matrons' Circle Building, a multiuse facility that includes a gymnasium, a theater, and music rooms.

Dr. Charles H. Green, who had served as superintendent of Griffin–Spalding County Schools in Georgia, was elected president of Tallulah Falls School by the board of trustees. He assumed duties on July 1, 1989.

The space shuttle *Endeavour* rocketed into the Florida skies at 7:42 p.m. on Thursday, May 7, 1992. *Endeavour*, suggested by Tallulah Falls School students, was the winning entry in NASA's Orbiter-Naming Program, which was created in honor of Christa McAuliffe, the schoolteacher who died in the 1986 *Challenger* accident. Georgia governor Joe Frank Harris recognized the school for this honor.

On May 16, 1989, Pres. George H.W. Bush presented an award to the Tallulah Falls School students who submitted a winning entry in NASA's Orbiter-Naming Program in a ceremony at the White House. That the students, faculty, and staff of Tallulah Falls School should be present for the shuttle's initial launch was only fitting, since a team of students from the school named it.

The current dining facility, Federation Hall, and the Lettie Pate Evans Student Center were dedicated in October 1996. Federation Hall was named in honor of the Georgia Federation of Women's Clubs, which founded the school in 1909.

The new student center that opened in 1996 was named in honor of Lettie Pate Evans, a friend of Tallulah Falls School and the school's most generous benefactor. Her legacy gift, administered through the Lettie Pate Evans Foundation, amounts to more than $10 million per year and is used to assist with the operation of the school and to provide scholarships to deserving students.

In February 1957, Nannie Woodward Westmoreland died and left her entire estate to Tallulah Falls School. In her will, she directed the school to construct a native stone dormitory to house around 75 girls. Westmoreland, built in 1959, serves as a home away from home for approximately 65 female students.

In 1961, Tallulah Falls School received a special honor when it was recognized as one of 35 outstanding small high schools in the United States. It was the only school in Georgia to be so honored. Also in 1961, construction began on the Ida Fitzpatrick Dormitory for boys, which was completed in 1963.

This is a view of male students in the Ida Fitzpatrick Dormitory around 1967. Today, the school has boarding space for 72 males and 64 females. Tallulah Falls School has served students from more than 20 countries, including Belarus, the Bahamas, Cambodia, China, the Cayman Islands, Croatia, Spain, the Republic of Georgia, Kazakhstan, South Korea, Mexico, Montenegro, Nigeria, Poland, Romania, Serbia, Turkey, Taiwan, Uganda, Ukraine, Venezuela, and Vietnam.

Transportation options around the school today are greatly expanded from the bus pictured here in 1967. Then and now, bus drivers are part of the TFS family and drive students not only to and from school but also to athletic events and on school trips.

Today, with 18 buses in its fleet, Tallulah Falls School shuttles students from five surrounding counties, making it possible for working parents to take advantage of giving their children a college-preparatory education.

This vintage classroom setting showcases how the student experience has evolved over the years. The slide rule this student is holding predates modern technology.

This image illustrates the school's continued commitment to the work program by showing female students working in the kitchen. The school's dining service was coordinated in-house for the majority of its history, with longtime director Harriett Worrell retiring in 2020. It is now outsourced through Flik Independent School Dining Services.

Snow days at TFS offer a chance to frolic and take a break from classes. For some boarding students from more temperate climates, it is often the first time they have experienced a winter landscape. The school maintains a supply of sleds for these days.

Tallulah Gorge State Park, operated by the Georgia Department of Natural Resources, is a popular destination for outdoor enthusiasts. (Courtesy of Kimberly Brown.)

Tallulah Falls School once owned property that is now part of Tallulah Gorge State Park, but the school sold it to the Georgia Department of Natural Resources in 1994. Because of its proximity to the school, it is often a destination for field trips, outings, and service projects. (Courtesy of Kimberly Brown.)

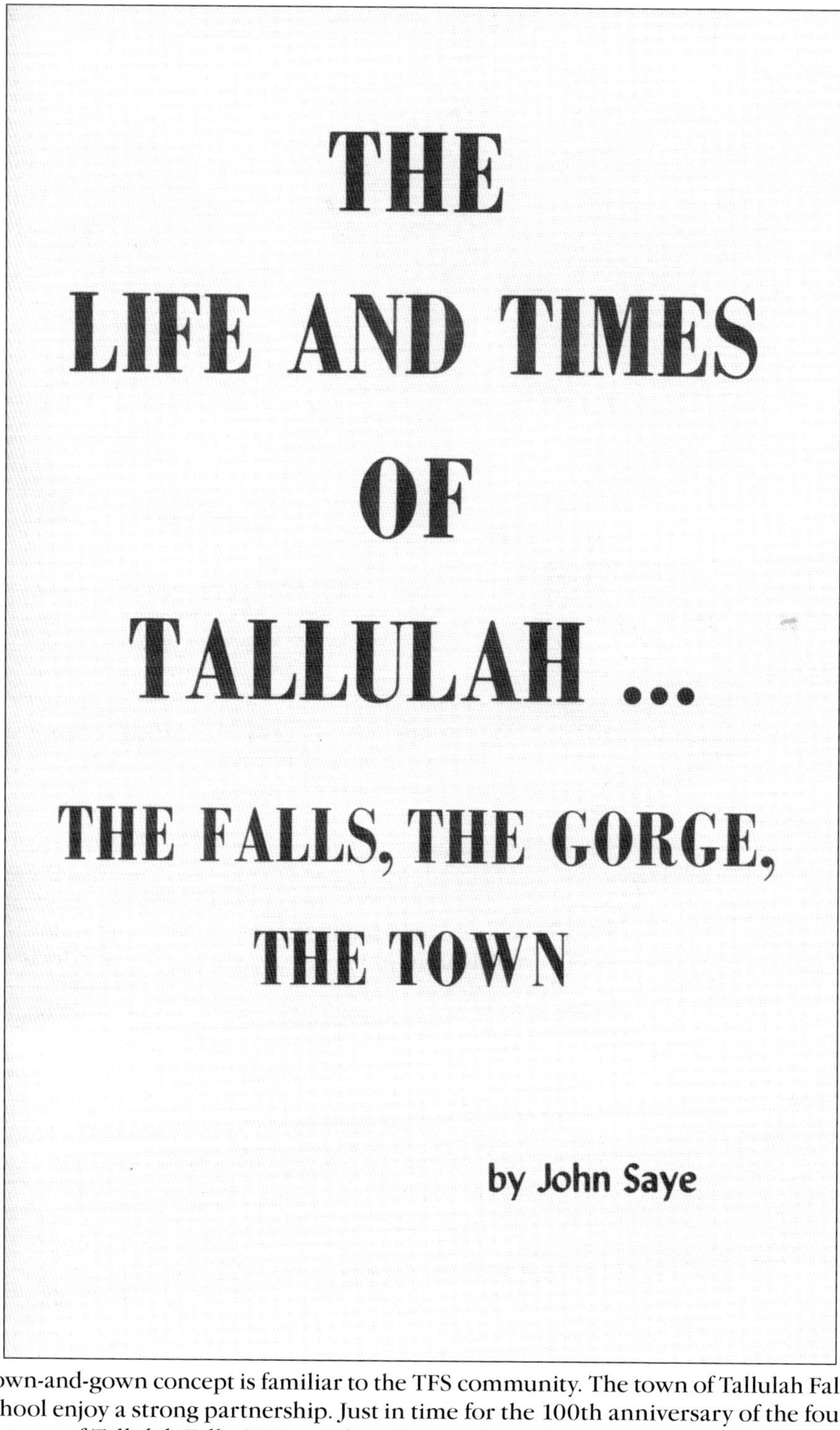

THE LIFE AND TIMES OF TALLULAH . . .

THE FALLS, THE GORGE, THE TOWN

by John Saye

The town-and-gown concept is familiar to the TFS community. The town of Tallulah Falls and the school enjoy a strong partnership. Just in time for the 100th anniversary of the founding of the town of Tallulah Falls, TFS social studies teacher John Saye wrote *The Life and Times of Tallulah* to celebrate the occasion. In a preface, then-mayor James E. Yon wrote of the preparation of the publication "for researching and writing this history of our community."

Four

Leadership Lessons

In 2007, Dr. Larry A. Peevy was appointed president and head of school by the Tallulah Falls School Board of Trustees. With a solid background in college administration, teaching experience, and boarding schools, Dr. Peevy was uniquely qualified to lead the school. His first task was to determine the state of the school, and working closely with faculty, staff, administrators, students, and parents, he implemented a SWOT (Strengths, Weaknesses, Opportunities, Threats) analysis. From this analysis, a clearly defined college-preparatory mission evolved: "Our mission is to prepare each student to thrive in life by elevating character and intellect in a challenging and diverse college-preparatory environment." From that unifying mission, all other successes have flowed.

Not wasting any time, Dr. Peevy set about a reorganization of the TFS facilities in 2007, giving the middle school a separate area and identity in the Cannon Academic Building by adding three new classrooms in the industrial arts shop area and using the original shop as a fourth classroom. Both upper school science labs were renovated, and industrial arts moved into an adjacent facility previously used by plant services. These upgrades were just the start of changes to come.

The 100th anniversary of TFS in 2009 was a yearlong celebration that involved present and past students, faculty, and staff; General Federation of Women's Clubs–Georgia (GFWC Georgia) members; TFS supporters; and local and state leaders. A special event was planned for each month. Highlights included an International Dinner honoring the school's students; a Business After Hours celebration featuring members of the Habersham and Rabun County Chambers of Commerce; a special 100th-anniversary presentation at the GFWC Georgia convention in Augusta; and the Centennial Finale during homecoming, including a Centennial Dance followed by fireworks. It was a time for remembrance and renewed pride in being part of a close-knit school community that has flourished for more than a century.

In 2009, 2014, and 2019, the school received dual accreditation from the Southern Association of Colleges and Schools (SACS) and the Southern Association of Independent Schools (SAIS). The facilities, curriculum, information technology, enrollment, athletics, and student life at TFS have taken quantum leaps forward under Dr. Peevy's leadership. The synergy among all of these facets working together has resulted in rapid and positive change; the whole truly is greater than the sum of its parts.

President and head of school Dr. Larry A. Peevy arrived on campus in 2007 during a time of transition at Tallulah Falls School. Under his leadership, the school has prospered. Many facets of the school's operations have taken quantum leaps forward far faster than the TFS strategic plan could have ever foreseen.

During the last 15 years, the school has grown by more than 400 students. Campus improvements totaling more than $40 million were put in place to enhance the student experience.

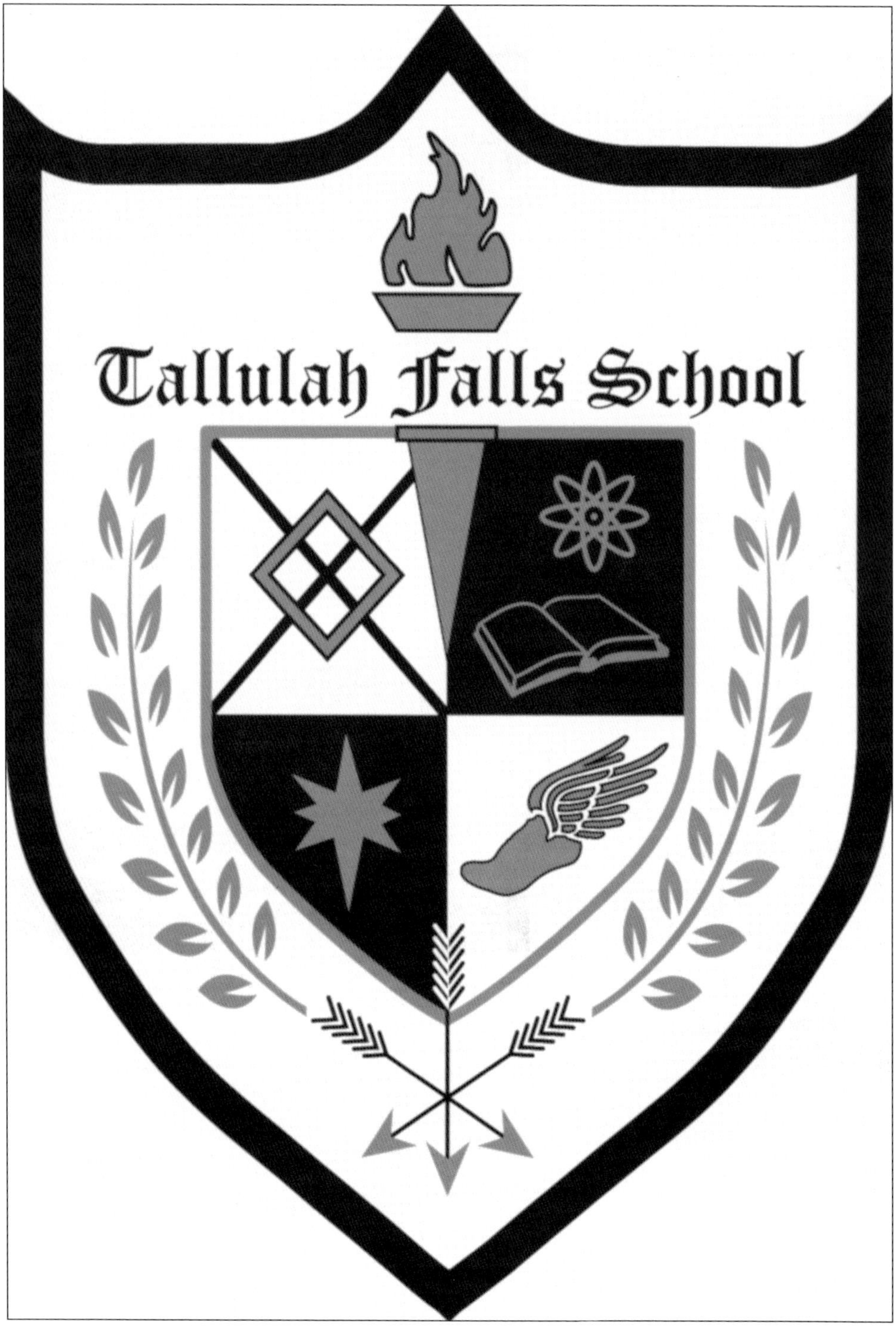

The torch on this crest symbolizes the Light in the Mountains, which has long been established as the school's tagline and purpose. The four quadrants represent (clockwise from upper left) character, academics, athletics, and spirit. The arrows represent light and life, and the white represents truth.

The Tallulah Falls School Board of Trustees is composed of local and state leaders, friends of the school, and representatives from the General Federation of Women's Clubs–Georgia. Former board chair Gewene Womack, a longtime supporter of TFS, is pictured during a special dinner.

This photograph shows the board of trustees' celebration of the early payoff of debt incurred in 2002 for dorm renovations at Tallulah Falls School. The school retired the $3-million loan for Westmoreland Hall and Fitzpatrick Hall as of December 17, 2019. Pictured here are, from left to right, former board of trustees chairwomen Amy Atkinson and Ellen Alderman, president and head of school Larry A. Peevy, former board chairwomen Carolyn Freelander and Gewene Womack, and current board chair Gail Cantrell.

There is a strong connection between Tallulah Falls School and the clubs across the state that make up the General Federation of Women's Clubs–Georgia. Today, GFWC Georgia club members support the school through financial means and board representation. The school issued a lifetime lease to GFWC Georgia for the use of the historic Lipscomb College as its state headquarters. Dinah Peevy, wife of TFS president Dr. Larry A. Peevy, extends hospitality to the club's members at the president's home when they visit the campus. Members of the Cartersville Women's Club are pictured here.

President and head of school Dr. Larry A. Peevy began a reorganization of the school facilities in 2007, giving the middle school its own separate area and beginning an extensive series of renovations and new construction. This momentum continues to build as major construction projects—the Student Activity Center, Higgins Baseball Complex, and natatorium—add value to the TFS experience. In 2011, the school came to possess the Lodge at Tallulah Falls, a 55-room hotel adjacent to the school farm property. After consulting with architects, engineers, and builders, it was converted into a separate middle school campus. Named for Lucy A. Willard, the complex opened for the 2011–2012 academic year. Willard is a member of the Atlanta Woman's Club and has contributed more than $1 million to the school.

In 2009, Tallulah Falls School celebrated its 100th anniversary with a yearlong celebration involving present and past students, faculty, and staff, as well as General Federation of Women's Clubs–Georgia members and surrounding local and state leaders. Activities and events that year included the completion of a historical timeline that can be seen in the lobby of the Young Matrons' Circle Building.

In addition to gaining intelligence via their studies, TFS students also greatly benefit from an innovative character development program that has been incorporated into academics, athletics, and boarding. All students learn the value of service beyond self, often through volunteering for a local organization or nonprofit, including helping at animal shelters, creating and delivering cards to residents of nursing homes, raising money and collecting supplies for victims of storms, collecting goods for the food bank, reading to students at an elementary school, or helping with various United Way service projects. Anna Paige Barrett (class of 2020) is shown with a furry friend from Paws for Life, the animal shelter in Rabun County.

Five

GAINING GROUND

Enrollment has more than tripled under Tallulah Falls School president Larry A. Peevy's leadership; it has grown from 120 students (a majority of them boarding students) in 2007 to 555 students at the start of the 2021–2022 academic year.

TFS was founded in 1909 to provide educational opportunities for local mountain children, and that founding mission is especially thriving in the present day. Dramatic enrollment growth on a scale of this magnitude—and at a time of economic flux—is highly unusual and can be attributed to multiple factors.

Parents strongly believe in the school's mission and its dual emphasis on elevating both character and intellect. The learning community responded positively when, in February 2013, TFS implemented an innovative tuition freeze in which a student's base tuition rate is locked in at the time of initial enrollment and remains fixed for all of that student's years at the school. Because the school is not tuition-driven (only about 20 percent of the school's budget is funded by tuition dollars), generous need-based financial assistance is available.

This has elevated the quality of students who want to be part of a school community where they are academically challenged. Word spread to surrounding communities about TFS's successes, and outreach efforts have resulted in a stellar school image and heightened local awareness of the school. Additionally, the school has top-flight admissions and communications departments and the vision to use those departments wisely and creatively.

Highlights from this recent period include the repurposing of the Lodge at Tallulah Falls hotel; creating a new, autonomous middle school campus; the completion of a new natatorium, the Student Activity Center (a multipurpose facility for athletics, performances, and special events), and the four-year expansion of the Larry A. Peevy Academic Complex; the dedications of the Dinah A. Peevy Equestrian Center and Higgins Baseball Complex; the addition of state-of-the-art technology, including laptops for every student, two Mac labs, virtual reality and Zspace for classroom lesson enhancement, and a wireless campus; offering 20 college classes on campus; maintaining a small classroom environment; a 100 percent college acceptance rate; a retention rate of 96 percent; $3.5 million awarded in financial aid each year; maintaining low tuition rates, which enables middle-income parents to be able to afford a top-quality college-prep education; a tuition freeze for all returning students in grades 5 through 12; and welcoming an international student body with people from 20-plus countries.

Over the past 15 years, increases in enrollment have driven the growth of faculty and staff. This image shows members of the 2019–2020 middle school faculty and staff on the first day of the academic year.

The majority of the faculty members hold advanced degrees in their subjects. For the 2021–2022 academic year, the school had more than 150 employees, making it a significant employer in the area. Members of the 2019–2020 upper school faculty and staff are pictured on the first day of the academic year.

Students are the heart of Tallulah Falls School. They are bright and motivated and hail from every corner of the state, nation, and world. They interact with faculty and staff to form a close-knit, extended school family. They are diverse, intelligent, curious, and accepting young people motivated to lead and to be successful. The class of 2021 is pictured celebrating their graduation.

TFS students do not just talk about character, they live it, volunteering for community service projects each year through the Interact Club, Key Club, National Honor Society, and other service groups. Two programs—the Tallulah 12 at the middle school and All In at the upper school—provide the framework for the character program. The class of 2021 is shown on College Day, during which students wear the colors or logos of the school they will attend after graduating from TFS.

Gilbert Gate is the original entrance to the school. It is now located across US Highway 441 from the main entrance that was created when the new road was constructed. At the time the gate was originally constructed, reaching it required a drive (or walk) of nearly one mile from the center of today's upper school campus. The gate, dedicated in 1939, is named for Justice Stirling Price Gilbert and his wife, Mary. Gilbert served on the Georgia Supreme Court from 1916 to 1937. Mary Gilbert wanted "an entrance worthy of the great work of Tallulah Falls School."

Today's campus is a blend of historic and contemporary, old and new, and has been carefully designed and meticulously constructed to create a unified theme that honors the original intent of its founders. In 2014, the school re-created an iconic image with female members of the senior class. As a "now" image shown next to the "then" photograph on the previous page, this picture marks the passage of time. Pictured here are, from left to right, (first row, standing in front of the plaque) Addie Aycock, Esther Adeyemi, Emma Fordham, and Celine Seguin; (second row) Betsy Bartholf, Hannah Gulle, Linden Pederson, Biba Roberts, Rachel Nichols, Isabelle Almoyan, and Madisen Gowan. These students also served as presidential ambassadors.

The events surrounding International Day, the celebration of cultural diversity at Tallulah Falls School, are highly anticipated each year. The day is marked by the sharing of culture, country-specific recipes, a performance showcase, and classroom activities. A day of service is also held in conjunction with International Day.

The information technology (IT) improvements at the school have been mind-boggling. All students in grades 5 through 12 are issued laptop computers, and computerized SmartBoards have been installed in all classrooms. A new wireless system has been implemented, increasing campus coverage from one building to nine buildings. The school's internet bandwidth has been upgraded tenfold, and the campus now has fiber connectivity. From left to right, middle school students Kalvin Ngov, Penny Damron, and Charlie Harris, are shown using Zspace.

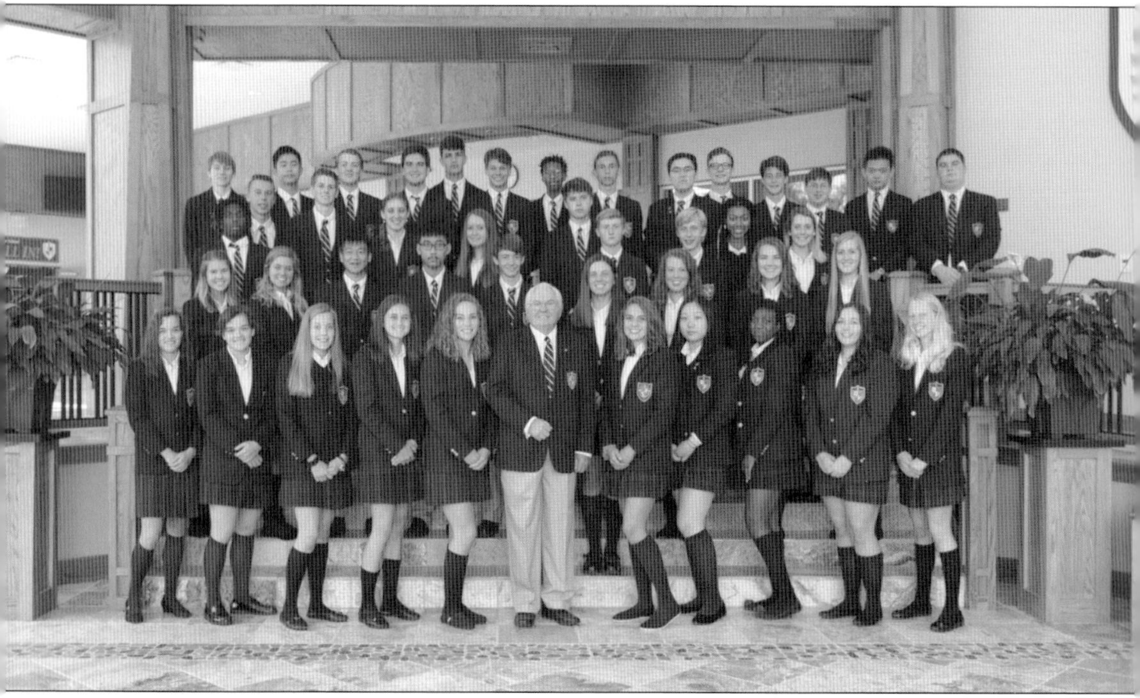

Student ambassadors serve as role models for their peers and project a positive image of the school on and off campus. Tallulah Falls School is also one of the larger employers in the area—with 150 full- and part-time employees, its faculty and staff members serve as additional ambassadors. This group of ambassadors posed for a picture in 2018.

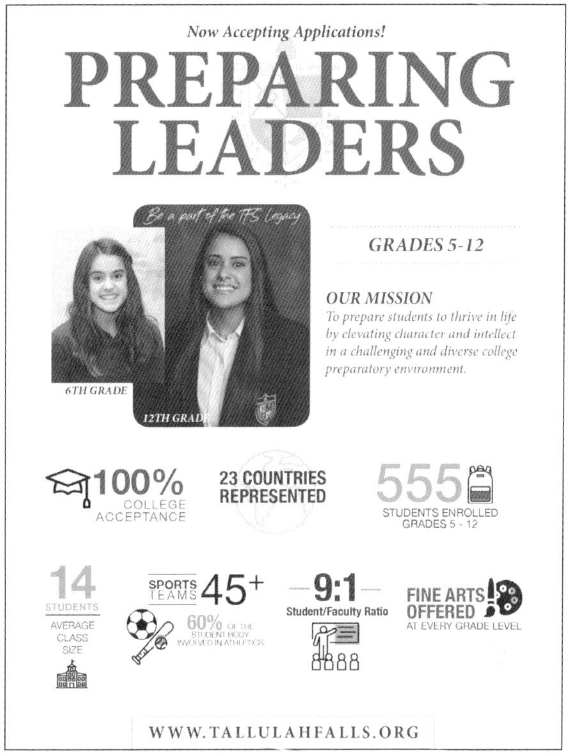

A recent admissions flier highlights the progress of the school's intentional enrollment management program. This process allows for thoughtful, consistent growth, fostering successful students and high retention rates.

Much has changed in the 100-plus years since the founding of Tallulah Falls School, but the school's commitment to the development of character and intellect remains steadfast. At the upper school, the All In initiative recognizes students in each grade for exemplifying a positive character theme each month. The All In Students for November 2020 are pictured here; they are, from left to right, freshman Addy McCoy of Cornelia, sophomore Henry Bowman of Cleveland, junior Flannery Hogan of Hartwell, and senior Simeon Respress of Cornelia.

Six

Building Boom

In 2011, when the school came to possess the Lodge at Tallulah Falls, a 55-room hotel adjacent to the school farm property, much discussion ensued about the best school use of the facility. After consulting with architects, engineers, and builders, it was determined that hotel rooms could, with the removal of walls, become classrooms, and—thanks to diligent work by Ron Cantrell Construction, Inc., and other contractors—the lodge was converted to a separate, beautiful new middle school campus in a few short months. The Lucy A. Willard Middle School Academic Complex was completed in time for the start of the 2011–2012 academic year. Lucy Willard is a member of the Atlanta Woman's Club and has contributed more than $1 million to the school.

Many campus facilities have been upgraded, including the Circle Building, the practice gymnasium, bleacher seats in the main gymnasium, the gymnasium floor, the theater (with new video screens and carpet), and the exterior of the building, which was spruced up with new awnings, doors, and landscaping. Just outside the Circle Building, a firepit and plaza have been constructed, providing a multipurpose gathering space. Federation Hall has enclosed seating on the porch and a new sound system and video monitors.

Willet Building upgrades include the construction of a trustees' board room, new information technology offices on the third floor, and a reorganized admissions area to better serve prospective students.

Two new state-of-the-art media centers have been built, including a media center management system incorporating an e-book checkout system. Digital textbooks have been integrated into the system. A scalable digital camera and mobile device synchronization system have been added. Multiple computers and peripherals have been added to the dormitories. The addition of two Mac labs, virtual reality, and Zspace for lesson enhancement bring additional tools into the classroom.

The natatorium, which opened in 2020, features a 10-lane competition-sized pool with seating for up to 240. The natatorium is home to the Tallulah Falls School competitive swim team and is used for physical education classes, including scuba, boating, and water-related safety courses. It is also open for recreational use for students, faculty, and staff.

The chapel was in dire need of a facelift, and new carpet, a new entrance and vestibule, and a new roof have greatly improved the building's appearance. A new climate-controlled server room on the lower level of Federation Hall has consolidated much of the information technology equipment in one location, facilitating maintenance and upkeep.

In terms of facilities, the school's $8-million upper school academic complex renovation project was completed in March 2014. The renovation added a new third floor to the academic complex with an additional 18,000 square feet of classroom space. A full renovation of the original two floors of the building has been completed and a new high-tech media center opened.

From a public relations standpoint, the appearance and functionality of this building, both externally and internally, have been transformed from a dated 1950s structure to a state-of-the-art technological 21st-century showplace. The academic complex is now, appropriately, the jewel of the school campus. In the fall of 2017, the board of trustees voted to dedicate the renovated facility as the Larry A. Peevy Upper School Academic Complex.

The Larry A. Peevy Upper School Academic Complex represents a four-year expansion of the original H.R. and C.R. Cannon Building. The three-story, state-of-the-art building is the main classroom center for students in grades 9 through 12. It features the latest technology in its media center and presents a dramatic impact for students, faculty/staff members, and campus visitors.

In 2016, the expansive two-story Student Activity Center opened on the middle school campus. The $6-million facility features a gymnasium, classroom space, a performance stage, a walking track, a 70-by-10-foot climbing wall, a state-of-the-art sound and digital display system, a fitness area, and outdoor gathering spaces, all completed on a pay-as-you-go basis.

The Student Activity Center is also the home gym for the volleyball and basketball teams. Both boys' and girls' middle school teams compete in the space. The facility also has flexibility for performances as well as everyday use for physical education, assemblies, and other activities.

The story of swimming at Tallulah Falls School spills forth from a deep well of history. Because of the school's location on the slope of Cherokee Mountain, the rich soil is saturated by natural springs, all running downhill. In late 2020, a new natatorium opened at Tallulah Falls School featuring a 10-lane, 25-yard competition pool and a Colorado Timing System, touchpads, and starter.

Additional features of the new natatorium include two large viewing monitors, one for times and the other for meet information; two areas for teams overlooking the pool; 18 monitors throughout the facility; and a hospitality room and concessions.

In late 2014, the school contracted photographers for a series of aerial images. While this view predates the natatorium, it is clear the school was thriving as it headed into the future. Located 90 miles north of Atlanta in the foothills of the Appalachian Mountains, the 500-acre campus of Tallulah Falls School is uniquely situated for outdoor recreation. Students enjoy proximity to Tallulah Gorge State Park and easy access to a variety of other activities, including hiking, camping, and snow skiing.

Seven

Promising Potential

In partnership with parents and guardians and the greater community, Tallulah Falls School (TFS) focuses on nurturing and developing students to their most significant potential.

TFS remains student focused and mission driven—a winning combination for any school. Thoughtfully compiled with input from all stakeholders, the school's strategic plan is not a finished document to be set on a pedestal and admired or tucked away on a shelf and forgotten. Instead, it is a blueprint for change that is subject to editing as future circumstances and opportunities dictate. These are indeed exciting times to be a part of the TFS community!

Mary Ann Lipscomb and the other founders of the school would be proud of today's students, who personify the traditions and spirit that have become synonymous with the TFS experience.

The 10-year campus master plan prioritizes major and minor construction and infrastructure projects on the campus. This forward-looking approach will ensure that prioritized projects match available funds with appropriate building locations to maximize campus site utilization and minimize costs.

With 100 percent of students accepted to college, it is with thoughtful intention that students are prepared for the next step in their educational journey. The recipe for success is simple: combine intelligent and highly motivated students with skilled teachers in a small classroom setting, add generous portions of personal attention in a close-knit family atmosphere historically associated with the school, and keep cutting-edge technology literally at the fingertips of every student.

The school's athletic program has also experienced remarkable growth and improvement in terms of facilities, participation, and outcomes. Today, more than 70 percent of students are engaged in more sports than at any previous time in the school's history. Growth has been especially significant in the middle school, with teams added to feed into all varsity sports.

A precision rifle program launched in 2017 is delivering consistent success. Class of 2021 graduate Samantha Stamey finished her senior season competing at high levels throughout her career. (Courtesy of Crump Photo.)

Middle school teams have been added in basketball, cheerleading, cross-country, golf, soccer, swimming, tennis, track and field, and volleyball. The varsity sports offerings now include volleyball, cross-country, soccer, basketball, cheerleading, swimming, tennis, golf, baseball, track and field, precision rifle, bass fishing, and E-sports. Anfernee Hanna of the Bahamas is pictured here. (Courtesy of Austin Poffenberger.)

The mission of Tallulah Falls School athletics is to develop GREAT character, competence, and competitiveness, to host GREAT events, and to create a season of significance. Here, GREAT is an acronym for Gratitude, Respect, Effort, Ambition, and Think. Denika Lightbourne of the Bahamas is pictured here. (Courtesy of Austin Poffenberger.)

The school's athletic program has experienced impressive growth and improvement. Shown is Sarah Jennings of Clarkesville. (Courtesy of Austin Poffenberger.)

Upgrades to the school's facilities include the construction of a new 100-meter sprint track, a walking track around the soccer field, two new tennis courts, a renovated baseball field and facilities, bleachers and the floor in the gymnasium, bleachers for the soccer program, a practice gymnasium, an enlarged and resodded soccer field, the construction of a home cross-country course, a student activity center, a golf performance lab, and a renovated weight-training room. All of these improvements elevate the student experience.

The Tallulah Falls School equestrian program started in 2010, and students are now competing in jumping, showmanship, and driving. Led by Dinah Peevy, an award-winning horsewoman, the student equestrians are following in her footsteps, garnering awards and accolades. The student riders work with various horses to deepen their experience by learning how to control horses with different personalities and temperaments; this allows each student to grow and develop in the sport.

Alumni success stories abound, with a plethora of recent contacts bringing reminders of the impact of the TFS experience. Rahel Gizhaw (class of 2009) is an Emory emergency medicine resident working at Grady Hospital, but she also rotates through Emory's different campuses as well as Children's Healthcare of Atlanta. Her resume includes a biology degree from the University of Georgia with medical credentials from the Morehouse School of Medicine.

In 2018, for the first time, a female track athlete from Tallulah Falls School won two state titles, and four former student athletes are currently competing at the collegiate level. Students are not only good athletes but good sports, winning regional sportsmanship awards in virtually every sport in which they have competed. Anna Davis is shown competing in the 100-meter hurdles at the Georgia High School Association Track and Field championships at Berry College. (Steven Eckhof of J and S Photography.)

Many TFS student athletes move to the next level to compete in college sports. On January 22, 2019, Virginia Griswold of Clarkesville committed to compete in swimming for the Smith College Pioneers in Northampton, Massachusetts. Pictured above are Nora (left), Virginia (center), and Kimberly Griswold. For the 2020–2021 academic year, the school hosted seven college signings. The 2021–2022 academic year is shaping up to be another banner year for next-level student athletes. Pictured at left is Montgomery Dampier, who will swim at Georgia Southern University. Dampier signed her letter of intent on December 2, 2021.

In 2014, the school launched the Twin Rivers Challenge, an annual cycling event held as a fundraiser for student scholarships. The ride takes cyclists through the breathtaking scenery of northeast Georgia. Riders come from throughout the Southeast to experience the school's warm hospitality.

The successful Twin Rivers Challenge cycling event and fundraiser makes it possible for more students to attend TFS, as it leverages community support through businesses, organizations, and individuals.

Growth has been implemented in incremental stages following a balanced enrollment management plan. Today, TFS finds itself with a retention rate exceeding 90 percent. Demand for student placements far exceeds supply. Pictured on the first day of the 2021–2022 academic year are, from left to right, Shelby Brightwell, Kenna Conner, Katriona Williams, Tilshon Leary, Tamia Moss, Alba Romanos, and Mara Radovic.

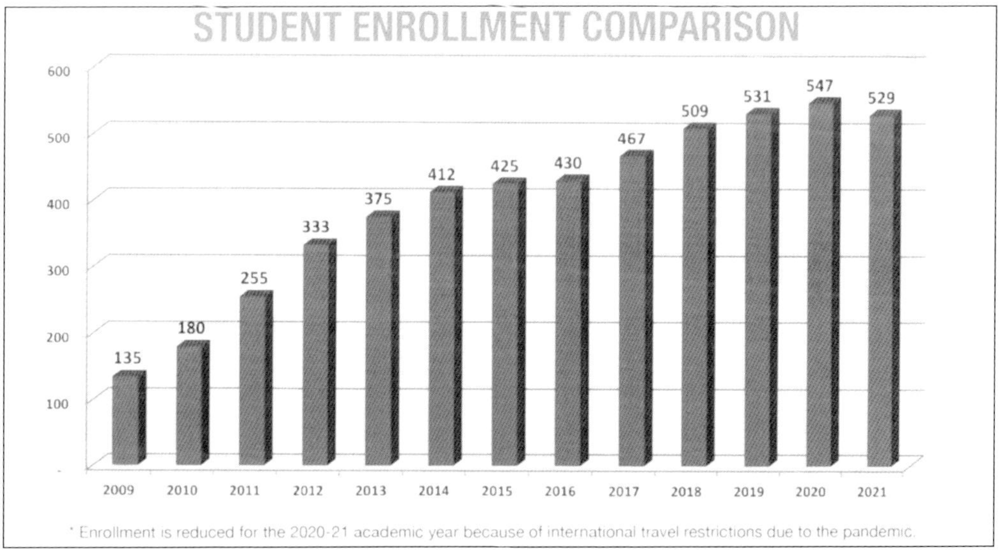

The past 15 years have seen fundamental change at Tallulah Falls School. TFS now has a well-defined mission; a growing, diverse, and immensely qualified student body; a caring faculty that is certified in their respective subject areas; a campus that shines with dozens of renovations and enhancements; a renovated academic complex; first-class athletic facilities, including a newly opened natatorium; established relationships within the surrounding communities; a thriving middle school; and a stable and thriving business model. The school's identity is crystal clear both on campus and in the surrounding region. Today, when people think of Tallulah Falls School, they know the school is college-preparatory in nature. TFS is well known for quality students, highly qualified faculty, and modern facilities.

The Tallulah 12 (T12) is the set of guiding principles the middle school uses to inspire character, confidence, and commitment. It focuses on the importance of relationships and community and the soft skills that often get overlooked but directly affect the success of students. It is designed to help students develop situational awareness; the school wants them to be able to recognize and assess situations in order to make well-informed decisions.

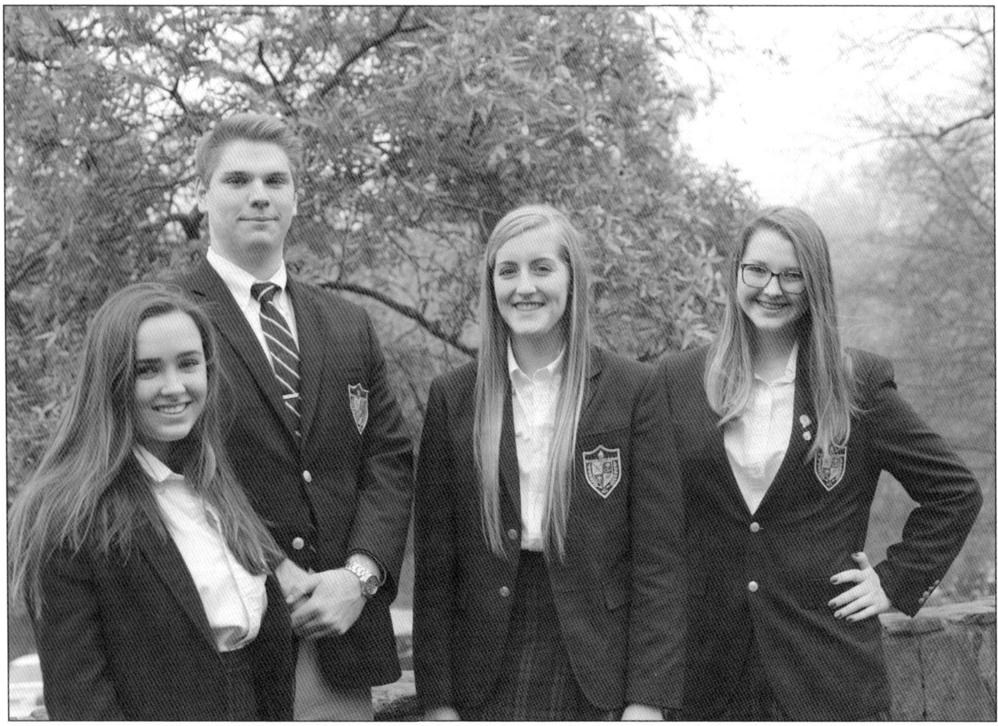

The school's focus on building character as part of its mission includes the participation of employees and students in local civic clubs, including Rotary, Interact, Kiwanis, and others. Pictured here from left to right are Manolin Santana, Matthew Weidner, Katie Corbett, and Madison Perdue—the Habersham Rotary Students of the Quarter for the third quarter of 2018.

At Tallulah Falls School, a focus on combining traditions from countries around the world creates a sense of community. TFS is a family, and whether one is from China, Serbia, or the Bahamas, all students are welcome. Flags representing the home countries for the school's more than 130 boarding students are displayed in the lobby of the Larry A. Peevy Upper School Academic Complex. The colorful flags offer a reminder of the diversity of the student body. In the 2021–2022 academic year, students from 22 countries attended TFS.

Stock Market Game Club members are shown with faculty advisor Kent Woerner, a county commissioner who was a regular substitute teacher at the school. The Stock Market Game Club is one of the diverse extracurricular options available to students. Shown from left to right are Chengxuan (Jonathan) Huang, Jun Kwon, Woerner, and Rui (Harry) Sun.

The student life experience is rich at Tallulah Falls School, with annual traditions woven into students' memory banks. River rafting; Atlanta mall visits; school trips to Chattanooga, Charleston, the Georgia coast, and Florida's Space Coast; and ski day are highly anticipated each year. Ski outings are possible because of the school's proximity to the slopes near Maggie Valley, North Carolina. Pictured above is middle school student Mallory Higgins of Cornelia, and below are upper school students Grant Barron and Gisella Welch.

Enrollment at the school has more than quadrupled from 120 students in 2007 to 555 students at the beginning of the 2021–2022 school year. Dramatic enrollment growth of this magnitude can be attributed to parents' belief in the school's mission and a dual emphasis on elevating both character and intellect. The Tallulah 12, a community-building initiative at the middle school, is part of this focus. At the upper school, the All In program picks up from the Tallulah 12, continuing the commitment to character development. From left to right are Benjamin Rosenthal, Cassidy Hayes, and Joel Bourlet showing off their house shield.

Longtime math teacher Linda Harris (pictured) is connecting with TFS alumni in a new role. Besides teaching math classes at the upper school, Harris is working with the advancement team as the alumni relations coordinator. She contacts former TFS students to update the school's mailing list—and more importantly, to reconnect with the alumni base. Harris has been at the school for more than 50 years.

In 2013, as a means of helping students' families, the school implemented an innovative tuition-freeze program in which a student's base tuition rate locks in at the time of initial enrollment and remains fixed for all of that student's years at the school (including any siblings who might follow them). Jenna (left) and Josie Chesser are shown on the first day of the 2021–2022 academic year.

Elective courses are well represented in the TFS curriculum, with course offerings that include art, broadcasting, computer applications, creative writing, culinary arts, drama, journalism, piano, strength and conditioning, chorus, and video production. Madi Perdue is shown during a drama performance.

Tallulah Falls School offers students a variety of clubs and activities, including a competition barbecue team. The TFS Pit Vipers finished the 2021 season as repeat state champions (in the Georgia BBQ Championship Series), reserve champions for the Southeast (Rufus Teague Series), eighth place in the KCBS Team rankings (Kansas City BBQ Society), and World Junior BBQ League champions. Shown from left to right are Jake Owensby, Joel Bourlet, Matthew Wolfe, Lily Turpin, president and head of school Dr. Larry A. Peevy, Brooke Hayes, Zach Freeman, Teryk Tilley, and head pitmaster Tom Tilley.

School uniforms were introduced for the 1997–1998 school year. Boys and girls wear khakis and shirts featuring the TFS crest. For formal occasions, students don a navy blazer featuring the school crest. Maria Whitson (left) and Paul Chambers are both members of the class of 2020.

The bedrock of any strong college-preparatory program is a challenging and stimulating curriculum. Tallulah Falls School offers 21 college credit courses to qualified students through a dual-enrollment program. This provides a valuable means for students to get an enormous head start on college careers and save a great deal of money. Honors courses are offered in all core subject areas—English, mathematics, science, social studies, and foreign language. Members of the class of 2017 are shown holding college banners.

It is a tradition at TFS to celebrate moving from the middle to the upper school. A class photograph, similar to what is done for seniors, is also part of this tradition. The class of 2025 includes, from left to right, (first row) Aiden VanOrman, Lizzie Huebner, Rylee Vandiver, Clay Kafsky, David Plaisted, Donovan Parnes, and Gavin Taylor; (second row) Jacob Mitchell, Koen Eller, Karagan Bransen, Emma Barron, Lily Turpin, Kalleigh Hartzog, Jace Ibemere, and Ava Hamon; (third row) Breelyn Wood, Kaitlyn McArther, Julia Smith, Emma Rose Hunter, Leah Rogers, Mallory Higgins, Kylee Loudermilk, Brooklyn Reed, Mia Hamon, and Madeline Martin; (fourth row) Landon Miller, T.J. Cox, Jedd Thomas, Chase Pollock, Zachary Woodworth, Will Greene, Tanner Davis, Noah Page, Lizzy Wanner, and Chesney Tanksley; (fifth row) Caroline Smith, Wyatt Franks, Raegan Duncan, Ella Akers, Mallory Higgins, Victoria Verberkmoes, Cindy Nwogu, Emmet Sims, Monil Patel, and Nicholas Edenfield; (sixth row) Timothy Beck, Ellenoir Adams, Hagan James, Millie Holcomb, Miah Gragg, Annelise Lance, Josie Chesser, Landry Carnes, Gemma Farris, and Kadence McMann; (seventh row) Jason Bard, Cole Borchers, Jake Owensby, Jackson Carlan, Teryk Tilley, Zachary Carringer, Zach Freeman, Jackson Cording, Jared Mullis, and K.C. Respress.

Bibliography

Hancock, Carol Stevens. *The Light in the Mountains: The Story of Tallulah Falls School.* Toccoa, GA: Commercial Printing Company, 1975.

———. *Not by Magic, But by Faith, Courage, and Earnest Work.* Toccoa, GA: Commercial Printing Company, 1982.

Various school newspapers, newsletters, magazines, scrapbooks, and other archival materials

About Tallulah Falls School

Tallulah Falls School is an independent, coeducational boarding and day school serving more than 500 students in grades 5 through 12. Academics and character development are at the heart of the Tallulah Falls School experience. The quality of the college-preparatory program and the success of students are the priorities that form the foundation of the school. For more information about Tallulah Falls School, visit tallulahfalls.org.

Discover Thousands of Local History Books Featuring Millions of Vintage Images

Arcadia Publishing, the leading local history publisher in the United States, is committed to making history accessible and meaningful through publishing books that celebrate and preserve the heritage of America's people and places.

Find more books like this at
www.arcadiapublishing.com

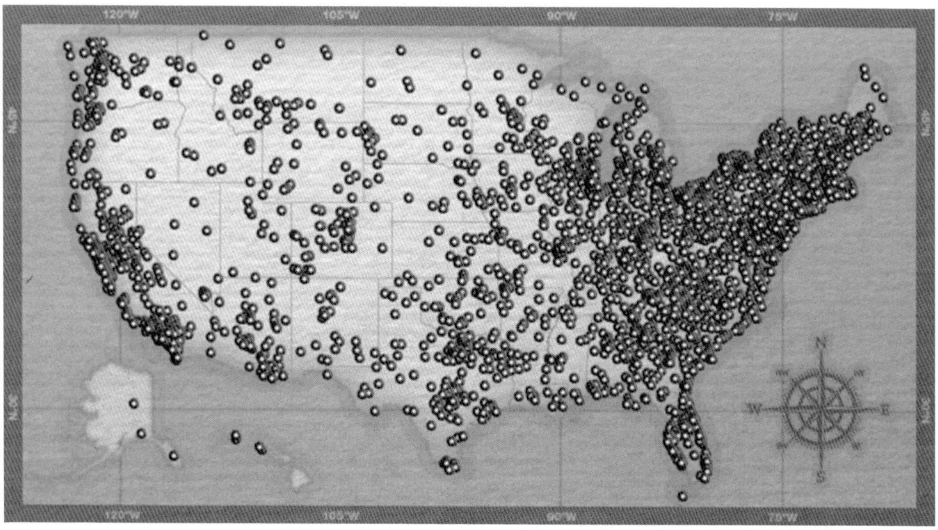

Search for your hometown history, your old stomping grounds, and even your favorite sports team.

Consistent with our mission to preserve history on a local level, this book was printed in South Carolina on American-made paper and manufactured entirely in the United States. Products carrying the accredited Forest Stewardship Council (FSC) label are printed on 100 percent FSC-certified paper.

MADE IN THE USA